COAL ENERGY

PUTTING ROCKS TO WORK

JESSIE ALKIRE

Consulting Editor, Diane Craig, M.A./Reading Specialist

Super Sandcastle

An Imprint of Abdo Publishing
abdopublishing.com

abdopublishing.com

Published by Abdo Publishing, a division of ABDO, PO Box 398166, Minneapolis, Minnesota 55439. Copyright © 2019 by Abdo Consulting Group, Inc. International copyrights reserved in all countries. No part of this book may be reproduced in any form without written permission from the publisher. Super SandCastle™ is a trademark and logo of Abdo Publishing.

Printed in the United States of America, North Mankato, Minnesota

052018
092018

THIS BOOK CONTAINS
RECYCLED MATERIALS

Design and Production: Mighty Media, Inc.
Editor: Megan Borgert-Spaniol
Cover Photographs: Shutterstock
Interior Photographs: Alamy; iStockphoto; Mighty Media, Inc.; Shutterstock; Wikimedia Commons

Library of Congress Control Number: 2017961847

Publisher's Cataloging-in-Publication Data
Names: Alkire, Jessie, author.
Title: Coal energy: Putting rocks to work / by Jessie Alkire.
Other titles: Putting rocks to work
Description: Minneapolis, Minnesota : Abdo Publishing, 2019. | Series: Earth's
    energy innovations
Identifiers: ISBN 9781532115707 (lib.bdg.) | ISBN 9781532156427 (ebook)
Subjects: LCSH: Fossil fuels--Juvenile literature. | Power resources--Juvenile
    literature. | Energy development--Juvenile literature. | Energy conversion--
    Juvenile literature.
Classification: DDC 333.82--dc23

Super SandCastle™ books are created by a team of professional educators, reading specialists, and content developers around five essential components—phonemic awareness, phonics, vocabulary, text comprehension, and fluency—to assist young readers as they develop reading skills and strategies and increase their general knowledge. All books are written, reviewed, and leveled for guided reading, early reading intervention, and Accelerated Reader™ programs for use in shared, guided, and independent reading and writing activities to support a balanced approach to literacy instruction.

CONTENTS

WHAT IS COAL ENERGY?

Burning coal

Coal energy is energy created by burning coal. Coal is a **fossil fuel**. It is formed from ancient plants. These plants were buried under dirt and water. This formed partly rotted plants called peat. Then heat and pressure turned the peat into coal.

Coal has energy. This energy is given off when coal is burned. Coal energy creates heat. It is also used to produce electricity. But coal is not renewable. Humans are using it faster than new coal can form.

Peat forms in swamps and other wetlands. It turns to coal over millions of years.

ENERGY TIMELINE

1300s

Hopi Native Americans burn coal to cook food and bake clay pots.

1769

James Watt patents a new model of **steam engine.** The engine increases **demand** for coal.

EARLY 1800s

Coal and the steam engine power the **Industrial Revolution**.

Discover how coal energy has changed over time!

1880s

Coal is first used to produce electricity.

1980s

Researchers begin trying to make coal cleaner.

2016

Coal is the second-largest source of US electricity.

HEAT AND STEAM

Humans have used coal for thousands of years. Coal was likely burned to melt metal in ancient China and Europe. The Hopi Native Americans used coal in the 1300s. They burned it to cook food and bake clay pots.

Coal became more popular in the 1700s. James Watt improved the **steam engine** in the 1760s. The steam engine was powered by coal.

Hopi pottery maker

JAMES WATT

BORN: January 19, 1736, Greenock, Scotland

DIED: August 25, 1819, Handsworth, England

James Watt was a Scottish inventor. Watt was repairing a **steam engine** in 1764. He noticed the engine was wasting steam. So, he built an improved engine. Watt patented his engine in 1769. It was used in mining and manufacturing. **Demand** for coal went up as the steam engine became more popular.

INDUSTRIAL REVOLUTION

Steam train

The **steam engine** powered the **Industrial Revolution**. Coal was important during this time. Ships and trains were the main methods of travel. These machines ran on steam engines powered by coal.

People also burned coal in furnaces and stoves. This provided heat for warmth and cooking food. By the 1880s, coal was used to produce electricity. Coal energy powered homes and businesses!

Coal burns at a higher temperature than wood does. Coal stoves are made of thick metal to withstand the heat.

CHANGING TIMES

Coal continued to be a main source of energy throughout the 1900s. But it has become less popular over time. Burning coal produces pollution. This includes **greenhouse gases**. These gases contribute to **global warming**.

Coal power plant

Researchers have tried to make coal cleaner since the 1980s. Power plants remove certain elements from coal. This reduces air pollution caused by coal.

One effect of burning fossil fuels is acid rain. This is rain that has been made acidic by air pollution.

HEAT AND ELECTRICITY

Paper manufacturing

Some coal is still used to produce heat today. But the heat is not commonly used to warm buildings. Instead, coal produces heat for manufacturing. The heat is used to make concrete and paper. It is also used in steelmaking.

Most coal is used to produce electricity. Burning coal creates energy. This energy is converted into electricity. It powers homes and businesses all over the world.

Power lines carry electricity from coal plants to consumers.

MINING FOR COAL

Coal is mined from underground. There are two methods of mining. Surface mining takes coal from near Earth's surface. Miners remove layers of soil and rock. This exposes the coal underneath.

Underground mining reaches coal deep underground. The mines can be 1,000 feet (300 m) deep! Miners take elevators down into these mines.

Surface mining

Explosions and falling rocks are common dangers in underground coal mines.

PRODUCING ELECTRICITY

Steam turbine

Mined coal is sent to a plant for cleaning. This makes coal more valuable. It also helps remove elements that cause pollution.

Most coal is then shipped to power plants. The coal is ground into powder and burned. The heat produced boils water to make steam. The steam turns a **turbine**. The turbine rotates a **generator**. This creates electricity!

COAL POWER PLANT

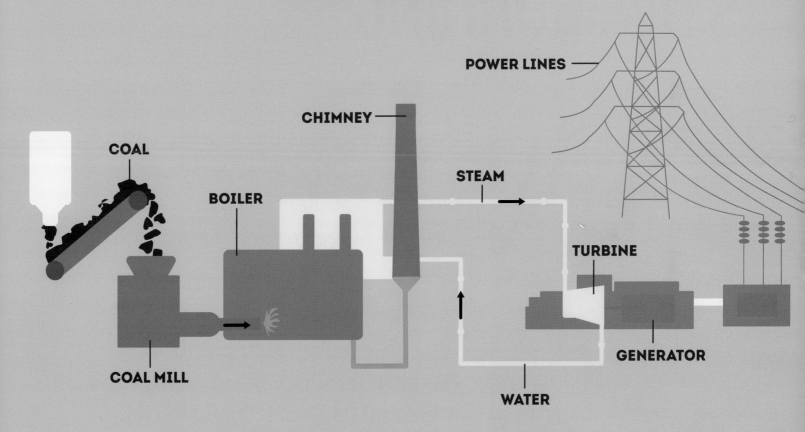

COAL

COAL MILL

BOILER

CHIMNEY

POWER LINES

STEAM

TURBINE

GENERATOR

WATER

STILL BURNING

Coal energy has been used less over time. Cleaner energies have become popular. In 2016, natural gas produced more US electricity than coal.

However, coal is cheaper than other fuels. It is also plentiful. **Researchers** explore new ways to mine and use coal. They also keep working to make coal cleaner!

Researchers today are looking for ways to use waste products from coal mining and burning.

MORE ABOUT COAL ENERGY

Do you want to tell others about coal energy? Here are some fun facts to share!

THE UNITED STATES has enough coal to last 200 to 300 years.

COAL is mostly made of carbon.

THE OLDEST COAL TODAY is about 300 million years old!

TEST YOUR KNOWLEDGE

1. Coal is formed from ancient plants. **TRUE OR FALSE?**

2. When did James Watt patent his **steam engine**?

3. Which type of coal mining uses elevators?

THINK ABOUT IT!

Are there coal mines or coal power plants near you?

ANSWERS: 1. True **2.** 1769 **3.** Underground mining

GLOSSARY

demand – the amount of a product that buyers are willing and able to purchase.

fossil fuel – a fuel formed from the remains of plants or animals. Coal, oil, and natural gas are fossil fuels.

generator – a machine that creates electricity.

global warming – an increase in the average temperature of Earth's surface.

greenhouse gas – a gas, such as carbon dioxide, that traps heat in Earth's atmosphere.

Industrial Revolution – a period in Britain from about 1750 to 1850, when power-driven machinery started being used to make goods.

researcher – someone who tries to find out more about something.

steam engine – an engine that uses boiling water for power.

turbine – a machine that produces power when it is rotated at high speed.